Team Strings

An integrated course for individual, group and mixed instrument teaching

Viola

Richard Duckett, Olive Goodborn & Christopher Rogers

International MUSIC Publications

Published by
International Music Publications Ltd
Griffin House 161 Hammersmith Road London England W6 8BS

Edited by BARRIE CARSON TURNER

Piano accompaniments by BARRIE CARSON TURNER

Sincere thanks are extended to the following people:
CHRISTOPHER BULL, author and arranger of ensemble TEAM STRINGS BOOK 1, for the original plan for TEAM STRINGS BOOK 2.
CELIA DOUBLEDAY, cellist, who worked on the material in preparation.
ANN GOODBORN, double bass tutor who worked with Christopher Bull on ideas for the original draft.
MONICA HERMOLLE, cellist, for her invaluable support in the preparation of these books.
BRIAN LESTER, Birmingham Instrumental Team, for his invaluable advise and support.
SHELAGH REID, violinist and teacher (Aberdeen), for her invaluable advise on technical matters and repertoire.
JENNY SMITH, violinist and teacher (Worcestershire), for her invaluable advise and support.
LORNA WINDASS, violinist and teacher (Addenburgh, Oxfordshire), for her invaluable support and help on bowing the material.

First published 2002

Music engraving and typesetting: Barnes Music Engraving Ltd, East Sussex TN34 1HA

Contents

Team Strings 2 Ensemble

TEAM STRINGS 2 ensemble material has been specially written so that it can be played by almost any combination of string instruments the teacher may encounter.

On each ensemble page there are three or four parts. The first is the melody and the second is a duet part. The third and fourth parts are either a bass line, a harmony part or a descant. Each piece can therefore be used as a solo, duet, trio, or quartet with or without piano accompaniment.

By allocating the parts to different instruments it is easy to create a considerable variety of mixed ensembles, from a simple duet to a full string orchestra.

Each piece which can be played in emsemble or with a piano accompaniment also has the option of a CD backing track.

In addition to this, each piece can be extended into a longer one by varying the textures in subsequent verses. This can be done by reallocating the parts, playing in unison, using pizzicato accompaniments, introducing solo passages, etc.

The following symbols have been used to provide an immediate visual identification:

  Pieces with piano accompaniment

  Ensemble page
(score included in ACCOMPANIMENTS book)

  Pieces which appear in the same place on the same page in all four TEAM STRINGS 2 books

Vln	Vla	Vc	Db

The box to the left of each arrangement or score indicates where each piece can be found in the solo instrumental books.

Introducing Team Strings 2

As in TEAM STRINGS, TEAM STRINGS 2 has been designed to meet the needs of young string players everywhere, whether lessons are given individually, in groups or in the classroom.

Musical variety

TEAM STRINGS 2 has been specially designed to follow the original TEAM STRINGS TUTOR, although it can be used to follow on from any beginner string book. It offers the same wide variety of musical styles as the original, but is further enhanced by titles from the world of jazz and blues supported by a three-part course of improvisation techniques.

Ensemble pieces

TEAM STRINGS 2 offers corresponding pages of music which can be played in harmony for mixed string ensembles, from duet right up to full string orchestra. From page 43 onwards, TEAM STRINGS 2, TEAM BRASS, PERCUSSION and WOODWIND naturally share much of the same ensemble material allowing it to develop into full orchestra. As the TEAM STRINGS 2 tutors contain 25 pages of ensemble, they are suitable for school orchestra, string orchestra, symphony orchestra as well as solo, duet and other small groups.

Flexible course

TEAM STRINGS 2 does not offer guidance on how to play or teach a string instrument but rather offers material which the professional teacher can use to structure courses for individual pupils.

National Curriculum & GCSE skills

TEAM STRINGS 2 has been designed to help meet the requirements of the National Curriculum for music. In addition to fostering musical literacy, 'Play By Ear' lines provide early opportunities for composition and improvisation. This aspect of TEAM STRINGS can be a useful starting point for these elements in the GCSE examination course now followed by secondary schools.

Comprehensive notes on the use of this series, scores of the ensemble material, piano accompaniments and approaches to creative music making are given in the accompaniments book.

Accompaniments

Accompaniments for selected solo pieces, and the ensemble pieces, are available in the Accompaniments book and on the CD.

Lesson diary and practice chart

Date (week commencing)	Enter number of minutes practised							Teacher indicates which pages to study
	Mon	Tue	Wed	Thu	Fri	Sat	Sun	

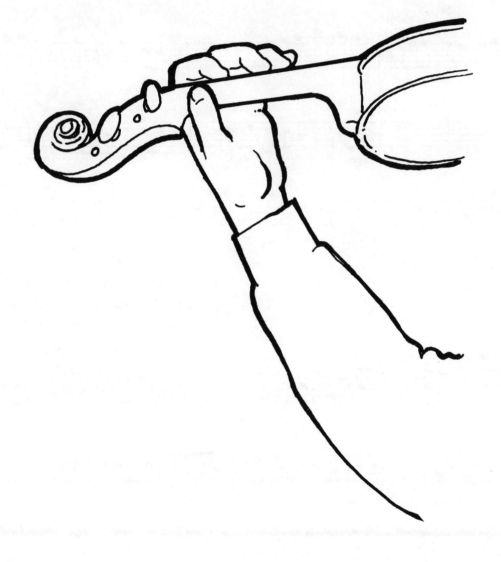

My grandfather's clock

4 clicks intro

Words and Music by
HENRY CLAY WORK (1832–1884)

The four dots mean
you can repeat the music
as often as you want

FLUTE

Moderately

3.

Moderately

4.

* Chime effect. Repeat chord 12 times, ad lib., and hold.

4

Heigh-ho

Words by LARRY MORLEY
Music by FRANK E. CHURCHILL

7 clicks intro

Simple gifts

Shaker melody

Daisy Bell

Words and Music by
HARRY DACRE (1860–1922)

6 clicks intro

rall. (rallentando) means
gradually slowing down

If you're happy and you know it

Traditional

Pattern

Compose a piece with the
same structure as *Pattern*

The Lincolnshire poacher

Traditional

Slur study

Melancholia

CHRISTOPHER BULL (1950–1994)

Key signature of E minor

My Bonnie lies over the ocean

5 clicks intro

Traditional

Staccato

Legato
means play the notes smoothly

Staccato
means play the notes short

Etude 1

Etude 2

Staccato duet

CHRISTOPHER BULL (1950–1994)

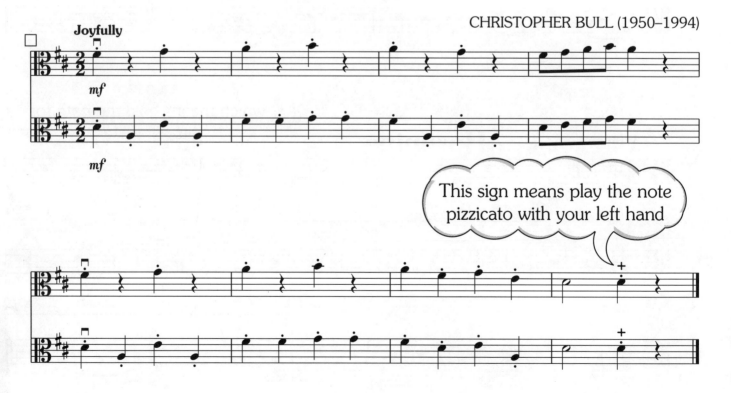

This sign means play the note pizzicato with your left hand

West Heath lilt

The cuckoo

EDWARD DUCKETT

Hornpipe

HENRY PURCELL (1659–1695)

Soldier, soldier

4 clicks intro

Traditional

Broken slurs

Das Blumchen wunderhold

LUDWIG VAN BEETHOVEN (1770–1827)

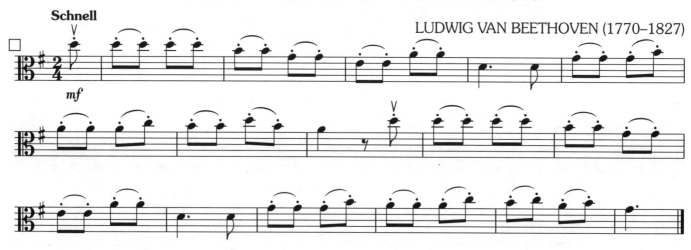

Sleigh ride

CHRISTOPHER BULL (1950–1994)

Study 1

German tune

Traditional

Allegro

Study 2

Minuet in G

HENRY PURCELL (1659–1695)

Moderato

Rhythmic decoration

Take it away man

16

Cockles and mussels

Traditional

Hoch Wass' kommt von draussen Rhein

Traditional

Play by ear

With a gentle rhythm

Fairly fast

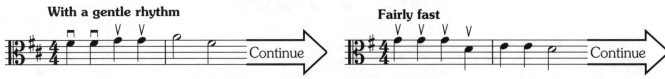

Sailors' song

4 clicks intro

Traditional

The key of D major

Music in D major has a
key signature of TWO sharps

L. A. nitespot
Twelve bar blues

Lasst uns erfreuen

Chorale melody

New world symphony

4 clicks intro

ANTONIN DVOŘÁK (1841–1904)

The rowan tree

3 clicks intro

Traditional

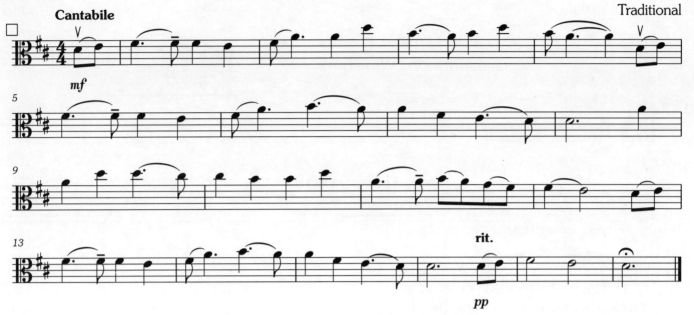

Swing low, sweet chariot

4 clicks intro

Traditional

Lullaby

5 clicks intro

JOHANNES BRAHMS (1833–1897)

For (s)he's a jolly good fellow

Three blind mice
Round

Frère Jacques
Round

Comin' thro' the rye

Traditional

Loch Lomond

Traditional

3 clicks intro

Scotland the brave

Traditional

4 clicks intro

play by ear

Continue

I saw three ships

4 ♪. clicks intro

Traditional

Joy to the world

4 clicks intro

GEORGE FREDERIC HANDEL (1685–1759)

1.

2.

3.

Melodic improvisation

When the saints go marching in

Traditional

5 clicks intro

After playing the tune you can
IMPROVISE over parts 2, 3 and 4

The key of C major

Music in C major has a
key signature of no sharps or flats

Scale and arpeggio of C major
(2 octaves)

Biddy Biddy

Traditional

Easy tempo

mf

mf

Look for scale
patterns

Round the scale

Abschied

6 clicks intro

Traditional

Intervals

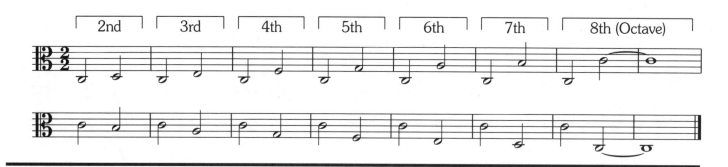

Study in C

Over the rainbow

4 clicks intro

Words by E. Y. HARBURG
Music by HAROLD ARLEN

Harmonics

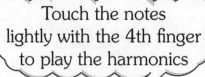

Touch the notes lightly with the 4th finger to play the harmonics

Pearls

Using the 4th finger
Top E

Step round

At a steady pace

mf

Whither blows the wind

Moderately

mf

> CROTCHET TRIPLETS mean that three crotchets are played in the time of one minim

> Play some of your tunes from Book 1 using 4th finger instead of open strings

Oh, Lady be good!

Music and Lyrics by
GEORGE GERSHWIN and IRA GERSHWIN

4 clicks intro

Slow and graceful

f

The keys of Canterbury

Oh, how lovely is the evening

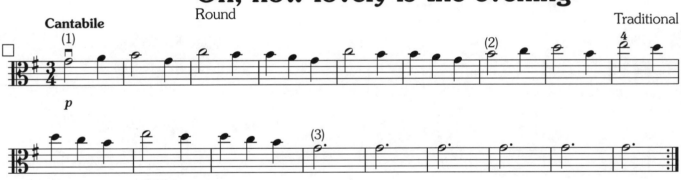

Polovtsian dance

Barn dance

Waltz from The Merry Widow

FRANZ LEHÁR (1870–1948)

6 clicks intro

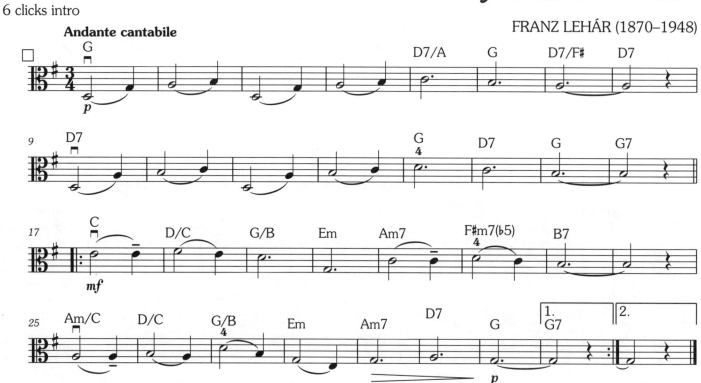

Oh! Susannah

STEPHEN C. FOSTER (1826–1864)

4 clicks intro

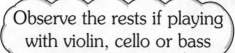

Scale and arpeggio of G major

Etude 1

Etude 2

Soliloquy

Camptown races

STEPHEN C. FOSTER (1826–1864)

4 clicks intro

Lively

mf

f

mf

COL LEGNO means tap the strings with the wood of the bow

Hickory, dickory, dock!

Traditional

Steadily

mf

Col legno

mf

Black Forest
Fits with *German Tune* in book 1, page 23

Summer's end
Fits with *Autumn* in book 1, page 21

Caribbean carnival
Fits with *Jamaican dance* in book 1, page 49

Marie's wedding

Joyfully

Traditional

Cindy

Cheekily

Traditional

Jubilante

Merrily

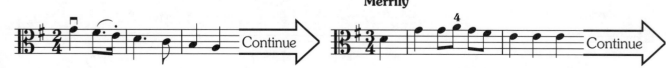

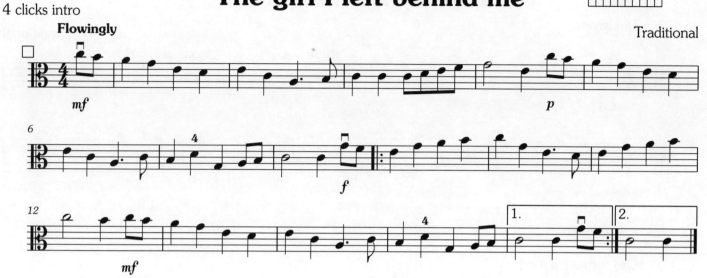

The girl I left behind me

Traditional

4 clicks intro

The northern lights of old Aberdeen

MARY WEBB

Hot cross buns

Traditional

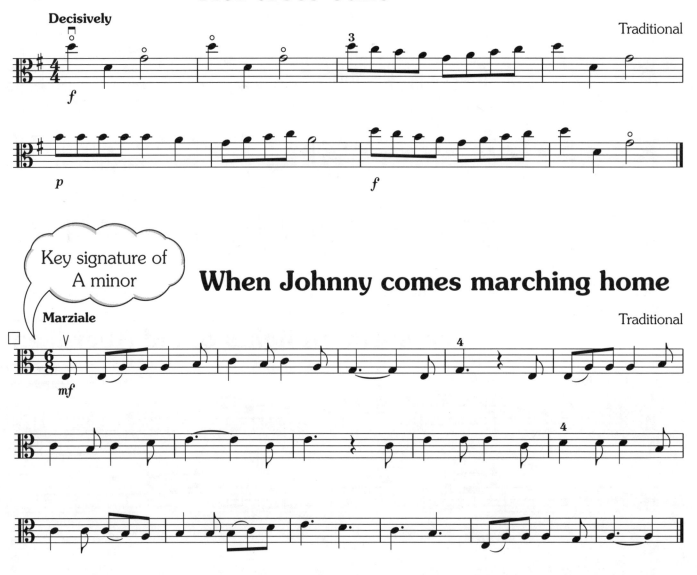

When Johnny comes marching home

Key signature of
A minor

Traditional

God save the Queen

Traditional

Believe me, if all those endearing charms

THOMAS MOORE (1779–1852)

5 ♪ clicks intro

The key of F major

The note B♭

Music in F major has a
key signature of ONE flat

The FLAT lowers the pitch
of a note by one semitone

Barcarolle

JACQUES OFFENBACH (1819–1880)

Slow waltz

Triste

Round

Make up your own tunes using
the notes G, A, B♭, C and D

Edelweiss

Words by OSCAR HAMMERSTEIN II
Music by RICHARD RODGERS

Au clair de la lune

Fits with *Au clair de la lune* in Brass,
Woodwind and Percussion books (page 37)

Traditional

4 clicks intro

play by ear

Upper B♭

Acapulco Bay

Fits with *Acapulco Bay* in Flute and Oboe books (pages 6 and 7)

4 clicks intro

Tempo de beguine

Slur round

Fits with *Step round* in Flute and Oboe books (page 8)

Steady

Skip to my Lou

Traditional

Playfully

Lullaby

Fits with *Lullaby* in Brass, Woodwind and Percussion books (page 14)

6 clicks intro

1.

2.

3.

4.

O little town of Bethlehem

Fits with *O little town of Bethlehem* in Brass, Woodwind and Percussion books (page 49)
This melody can also be used with the accompaniment part in Team Strings book 1 (page 45)

3 clicks intro

Traditional

Scale and arpeggio of F major

Little boy blue

Traditional

With a lilt

Fight the good fight

JOHN L. HATTON (1808–1886)

Brightly

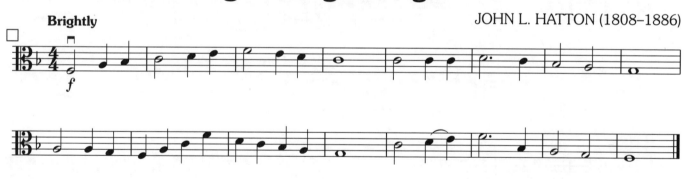

Liza Jane

4 clicks intro

Breezily

Traditional

Pentatonic improvisation

Pentatonic scale
on D

Question and answer
Using the pentatonic scale on D

Continue

Continue

I know the Lord's laid his hands on me

Traditional

Caribbean dance

The key of B♭ major

The notes Low E♭, E♭ & Upper E♭

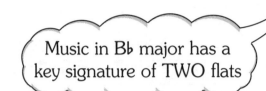

Music in B♭ major has a key signature of TWO flats

Quick march

March tempo

By nine year old REBECKA ELEY

John Brown's body

Traditional

Marziale

Scale and arpeggio of B♭ major

Little donkey

Fits with *Little donkey* in Brass, Woodwind and Percussion books (page 37)

Words and Music by ERIC BOSWELL

4 clicks intro

Pomp and circumstance

EDWARD ELGAR (1857–1934)

Blowin' in the wind

Fits with *Blowin' in the wind* in Brass, Woodwind and Percussion books (page 21)

4 clicks intro

Words and Music by BOB DYLAN

Third position

The magic carpet

Fits with *The wizard* in Team Strings book 1 (page 43)

Etude

The notes high F#
and high G

High F#

High G

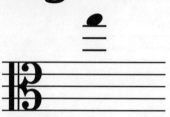

Pease pudding hot

Moderately

mf

Traditional

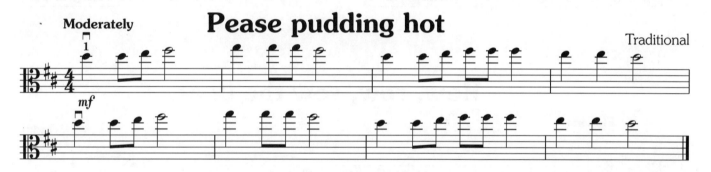

Scale and arpeggio of G major (2 octaves)

Song and dance

Fits with *Song and dance* in Team Strings book 1 (page 26)

Bright and rhythmic

Traditional

The key of A major

Music in A major has a
key signature of THREE sharps

Low C♯

Row, row, row the boat

Round

Traditional

Flowing

Shortnin' bread

4 clicks intro

Traditional

D.C. al Fine

The note G#

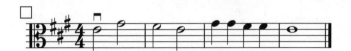

Scale and arpeggio of A major

All made up

Victorian ballad

Auld lang syne

4 clicks intro

Traditional

Hoe down

Molly Wicks and the pupils
of Greenmeadow Junior School

4 clicks intro

Scale and arpeggio of D minor harmonic

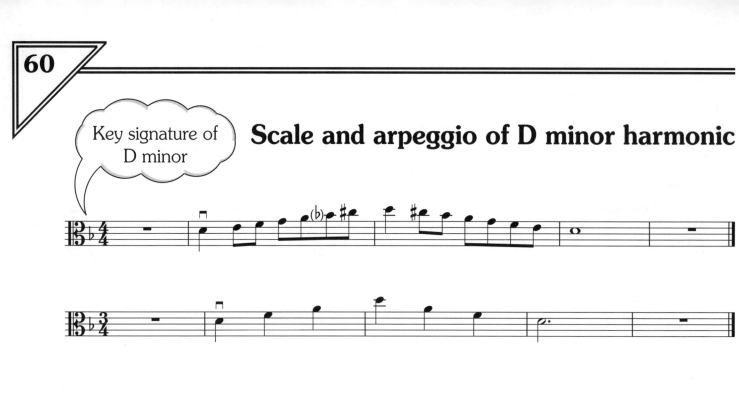

D minor round

The truth from above

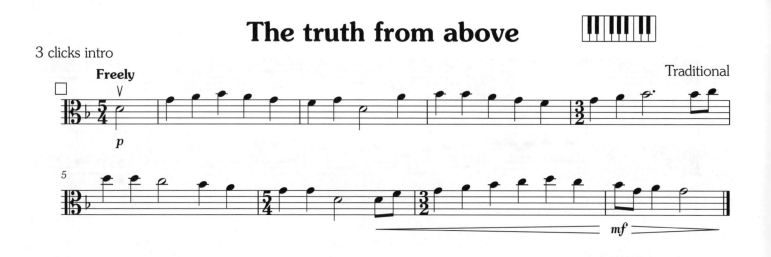

Charlie is my darling

Key signature of G minor

Scale and arpeggio of G minor harmonic

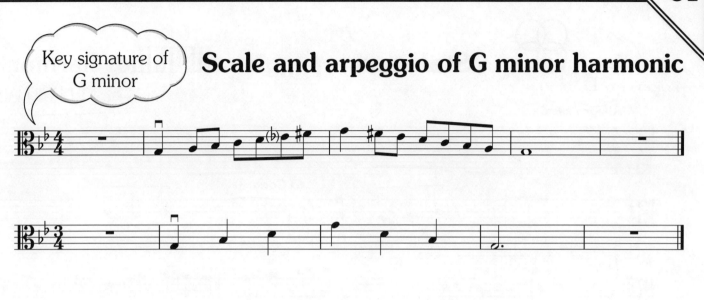

Coventry carol

3 clicks intro

Traditional

Summertime

6 clicks intro

Music and Lyrics by GEORGE GERSHWIN, DOROTHY
and DEBOSE HEYWARD and IRA GERSHWIN

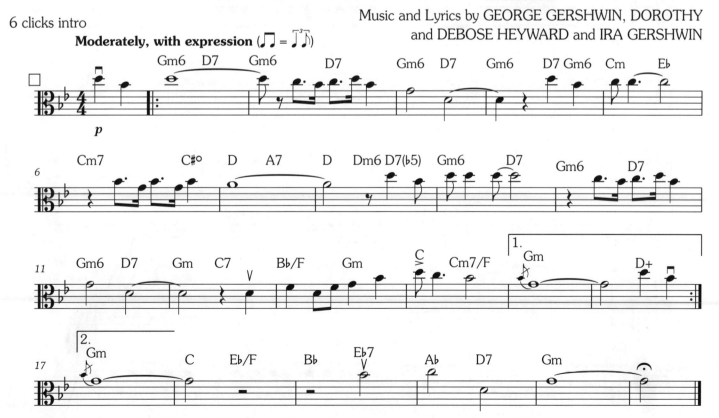

Star wars

JOHN WILLIAMS

4 clicks intro

My heart will go on

Love theme from *Titanic*

Words by W. JENNINGS
Music by JAMES HORNER

4 clicks intro

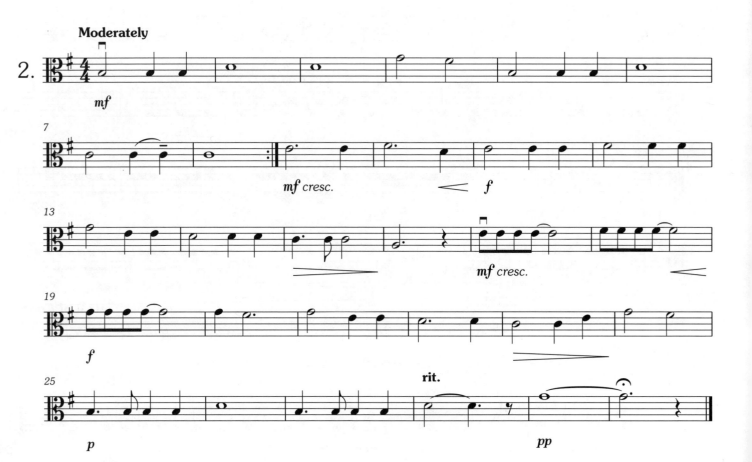

3.

Eternal Father, strong to save

Words by W. WHITING
Music by J.B. DYKES (1823–1876)

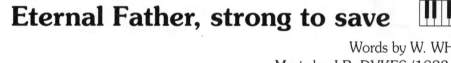

3 clicks intro

Pink Panther

HENRY MANCINI

7 clicks intro